AF599456

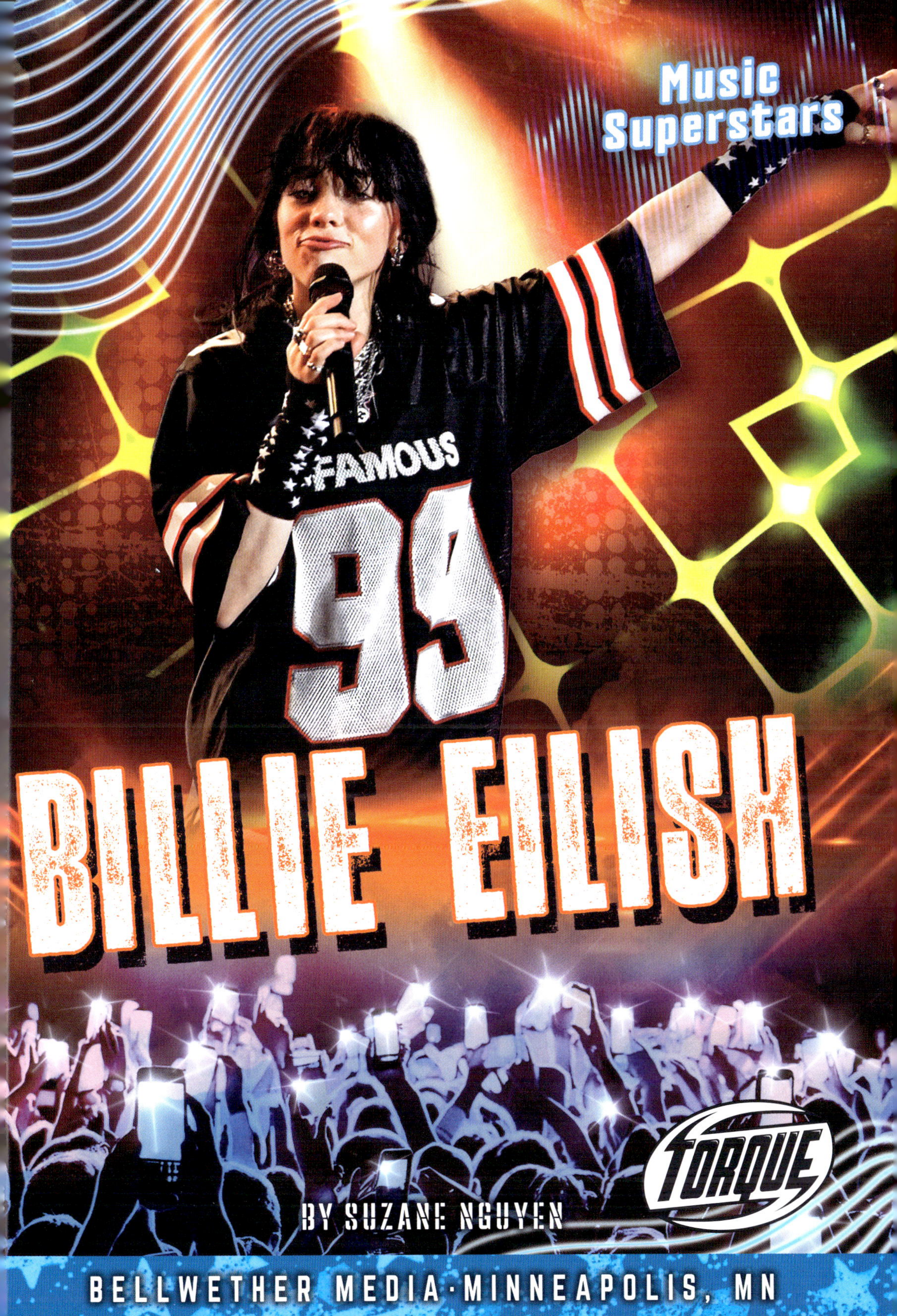
Music Superstars
FAMOUS
99
BILLIE EILISH
TORQUE
BY SUZANE NGUYEN
BELLWETHER MEDIA · MINNEAPOLIS, MN

Torque brims with excitement perfect for thrill-seekers of all kinds. Discover daring survival skills, explore uncharted worlds, and marvel at mighty engines and extreme sports. In *Torque* books, anything can happen. Are you ready?

This edition first published in 2025 by Bellwether Media, Inc.

Library of Congress Cataloging-in-Publication Data

Names: Nguyen, Suzane, author.
Title: Billie Eilish / by Suzane Nguyen.
Description: Minneapolis, MN : Bellwether Media, 2025. | Series: Music superstars | Includes bibliographical references and index. | Audience: Ages 7-12 | Audience: Grades 4-6 | Summary: "Engaging images accompany information about Billie Eilish. The combination of high-interest subject matter and light text is intended for students in grades 3 through 7"– Provided by publisher.
Identifiers: LCCN 2024046998 (print) | LCCN 2024046999 (ebook) | ISBN 9798893042627 (library binding) | ISBN 9798893043594 (ebook)
Subjects: LCSH: Eilish, Billie, 2001–Juvenile literature. | Singers–United States–Biography–Juvenile literature. | LCGFT: Biographies.
Classification: LCC ML3930.E35 N48 2025 (print) | LCC ML3930.E35 (ebook) | DDC 782.42164092 [B]–dc23/eng/20241008
LC record available at https://lccn.loc.gov/2024046998
LC ebook record available at https://lccn.loc.gov/2024046999

Editor: Rachael Barnes Designer: Josh Brink

Printed in the United States of America, North Mankato, MN.

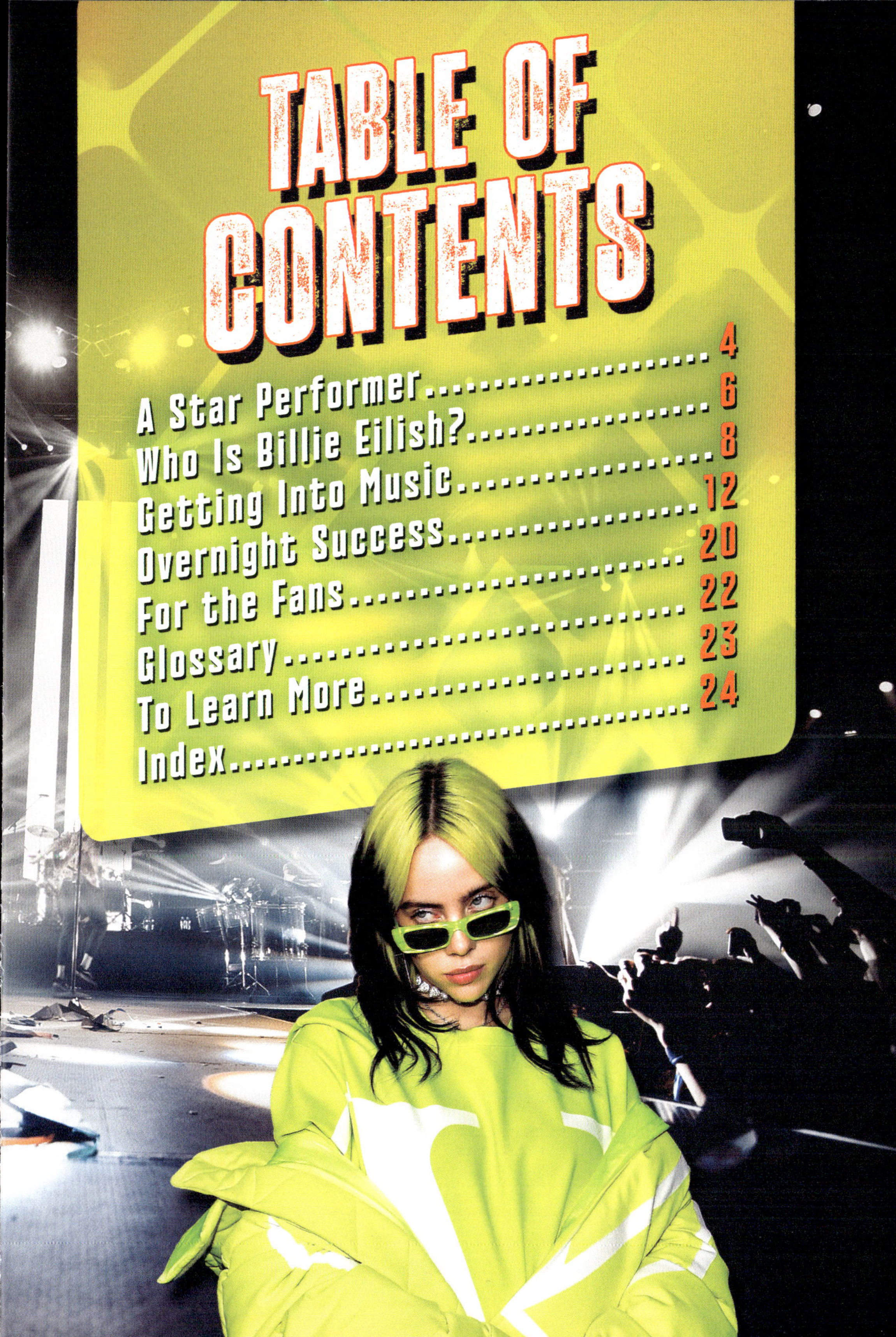

TABLE OF CONTENTS

A STAR PERFORMER

It is the 2024 **Academy Awards**. The curtains rise as Billie Eilish begins to sing "What Was I Made For?" Her brother, Finneas, plays the piano next to her. The stage spins to face the crowd.

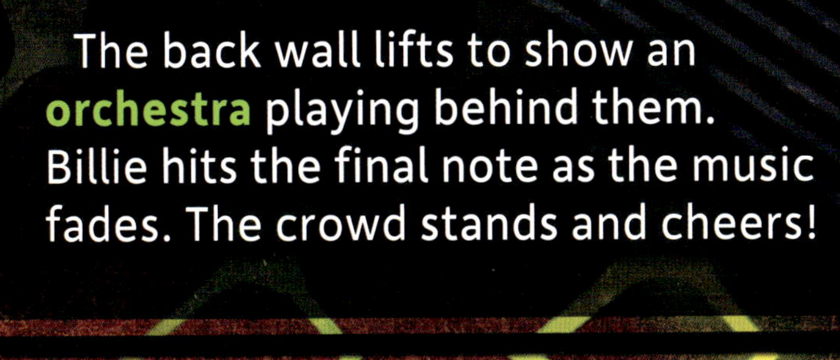

The back wall lifts to show an **orchestra** playing behind them. Billie hits the final note as the music fades. The crowd stands and cheers!

2024 ACADEMY AWARDS

WHO IS BILLIE EILISH?

Billie Eilish is a singer and songwriter. As a successful artist from a young age, she has set several world records. She has won many awards, including **Grammy Awards** and Academy Awards.

2020 GRAMMY AWARDS

Birthday
December 18, 2001

Hometown
Los Angeles, California

Type of Music
pop

First Hit
"Ocean Eyes"

Billie has created songs for big movies such as *No Time to Die* and *Barbie*. Starting in 2024, her seventh **headlining** tour featured her album, *HIT ME HARD AND SOFT*.

GETTING INTO MUSIC

BILLIE AND FINNEAS IN 2017

Billie grew up making music. She and Finneas were homeschooled together. They were encouraged to be creative and follow their interest in music!

At age 6, Billie learned how to play the ukulele. She joined the Los Angeles Children's Chorus when she was 8. Billie also took dance and horseback riding lessons.

BIEBER FAN

Billie is a big fan of Justin Bieber. They met in 2019 and are now good friends!

When she was 11, Billie began to write her own songs. She kept dancing, too! A few years later, Billie's dance teacher asked her and Finneas to make an original song to use for an upcoming show.

FAVORITES

TV Show
The Office

Snack
peanut butter pretzels

Artist
Lana Del Ray

Pet
tarantula

Finneas had a song in mind that he wrote. He and Billie practiced and recorded it together. They called the song "Ocean Eyes."

OVERNIGHT SUCCESS

TIMELINE

– 2016 –

Billie officially releases "Ocean Eyes" and signs with a record label

– 2017 –

Billie releases her first EP, *dont smile at me*

In 2015, Billie and Finneas uploaded "Ocean Eyes" onto **Soundcloud**. The song was officially **released** in 2016. It went **viral**!

The song's success helped Billie sign with a **record label**. In 2017, she released her first **EP** called *dont smile at me*. The EP shot to number 14 on the ***Billboard*** 200 chart.

– 2019 –
Billie releases her first album, *WHEN WE FALL ASLEEP, WHERE DO WE GO?*

– 2021 –
Billie wins a Grammy for Record of the Year for the song "everything i wanted"

– 2024 –
Billie releases her album *HIT ME HARD AND SOFT*

In 2019, she released her first full-length album called *WHEN WE ALL FALL ASLEEP, WHERE DO WE GO?* It earned Billie five Grammys!

Two of her Grammys were for the song "bad guy." It has gone on to sell over 10 million copies. Later that year, Billie released "No Time to Die" for the 2021 James Bond movie.

THE PLANT DIET

Billie eats only plant-based foods. She has been a vegan since she was 12 years old.

AWARDS
as of October 2024
7 MTV Video Music Awards
2 Teen Choice Awards
9 Grammy Awards
2 Academy Awards
2021 GRAMMY AWARDS

In 2021, a **documentary** about Billie was released called *Billie Eilish: The World's A Little Blurry*. Billie shared her struggles with her **mental health**.

The same year, Billie's second album came out. It was called *Happier Than Ever*. Many music organizations named it one of the best albums of 2021.

DISNEY ARTIST

Billie and Finneas have worked with Disney! They wrote "Nobody Like U" and other songs for the 2022 movie *Turning Red*.

Billie released "What Was I Made For?" in 2023 for the movie *Barbie*. The song won several major awards, including an Academy Award!

YOUNG ACHIEVER

Billie is the youngest person to win the Grammy for Album of the Year!

HIT ME HARD AND SOFT: THE TOUR

Billie released her album called *HIT ME HARD AND SOFT* in May 2024. The album had 72.7 million **streams** on the first day alone.

FOR THE FANS

Billie's music connects with many people and shares powerful messages. She makes it known how much her fans mean to her. When she gets on stage, her energy makes fans go crazy.

FASHIONISTA

Billie has her own clothing line called blohsh.

Billie continues to make a name for herself in the music world. Fans cannot wait to hear what she creates next!

GLOSSARY

Academy Awards—yearly awards presented for achievements in film; Academy Awards are also called Oscars.

Billboard—related to a well-known music news magazine and website that ranks songs and albums

documentary—a movie or TV show that tells facts about real topics

EP—a music recording that is shorter than an album but has more songs than a single; EP stands for extended playlist.

Grammy Awards—yearly awards given by the Recording Academy of the United States for achievements in music; Grammy Awards are also called Grammys.

headlining—related to performing as the main act at a concert

mental health—the way people think and feel about themselves and the world around them

orchestra—a group of musicians performing instrumental music

record label—a company that sells music

released—made music available for listening

Soundcloud—a streaming platform used for uploadin and listening to music, especially from new or independent artists

streams—listens or plays online

viral—popular from being shared quickly

TO LEARN MORE

AT THE LIBRARY

Bell, Samantha. *Billie Eilish.* New York, N.Y.: Crabtree Publishing, 2025.

Borgert-Spaniol, Megan. *Billie Eilish: Singing Superstar.* Minneapolis, Minn.: Abdo Publishing, 2022.

Schwartz, Heather E. *Billie Eilish: Chart-Topping Artist.* Minneapolis, Minn.: Lerner Publications, 2023.

ON THE WEB

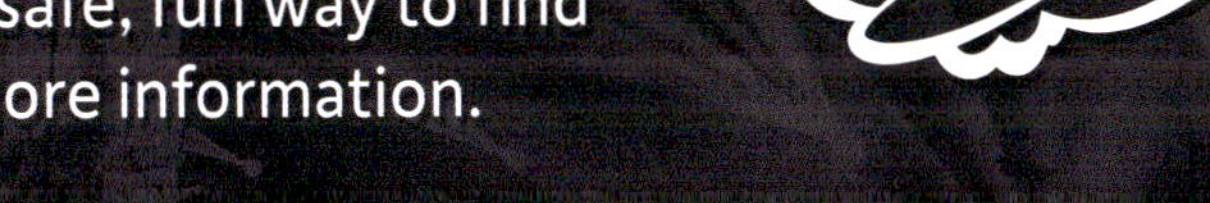

Factsurfer.com gives you a safe, fun way to find more information.

1. Go to www.factsurfer.com.
2. Enter "Billie Eilish" into the search box and click 🔍.
3. Select your book cover to see a list of related content.

INDEX

The images in this book are reproduced through the courtesy of: Didier Messens/ Getty Images, front cover (Billie Eilish); Catsense, front cover (lights); Taya Ovod, pp. 2-3; DFree, p. 3; Kevin Winter/ Getty Images, pp. 4-5, 5; Steve Granitz/ Getty Images, p. 6; C Flanigan/ imageSPACE/ Alamy, p. 7 (infographic); Chris Pizzello/ Invision/ AP Newsroom, p. 7; Omar Vega/ Invision/ AP Newsroom, p. 8; Lorne Thomson/ Redferns/ Getty Images, p. 9; Amy Harris/ Invision/ AP Newsroom, p. 10; Rob Grabowski/ Invision/ AP Newsroom, p. 11; Photo12/NBC Universal Television/ Alamy, p. 11 (*The Office*); Elizabeth A.Cummings, p. 11 (peanut butter pretzels); Justin Higuchi/ Wikipedia, p. 11 (Lana Del Rey); Marjan Madyansyah, p. 11 (tarantula); Rob Latour/ Variety/ Penske Media/ Getty Images, pp. 12-13; Dabarti CGI, pp. 12-13 (timeline mixing board); jbrink, pp. 12-13, 21 (playlist); Rebecca Sapp/ WireImage/ Getty Images, p. 14; WFDJ_Stock, p. 15 (MTV Video Music Awards); CarlosVdeHabsburgo/ Wikipedia, p. 15 (Grammy Awards); Featureflash Photo Agency, p. 15 (Teen Choice Awards); AlexanDior, p. 15 (Academy Awards); Kevin Mazur/ Getty Images, pp. 15, 19, 21; Koury Angelo/ Getty Images, p. 16; TCD/ Prod.DB/ Alamy, p. 17; Jordan Strauss/ Invision/ AP Newsroom, p. 18; Jun Sato/ WireImage/ Getty Images, p. 20; Christian Bertrand, p. 23.